Argentina Travel Guide

A Guidebook to Explore Buenos Aires, Wine Country, and Much More in This Beautiful Country

By

Yasdey Rojas

TABLE OF CONTENTS

AN INTRODUCTION TO THE HISTORY OF ARGENTINA

Located below the southern half of the continent, Argentina is the most visited country in South America, largely due to its prime location next to Bolivia, Paraguay, Uruguay, and Chile. While the country is mostly bordered by the Andean mountain range to the west, its eastern border is primarily comprised of coastal land that borders the South Atlantic Ocean. With land mass sufficient enough to be named the fourth-largest country in South America, Argentina is the eighth-largest country in the world and is the largest country within South America that uses Spanish as its primary speaking language. With twenty-three provinces dividing the country, Argentina's government is comprised of a federal government that also controls various territories such as the Falkland Islands and the country's claim in Antarctica.

Argentina's history is rich, dating to prehistoric times with the first recorded inhabitants being alive during the Paleolithic Period. Similar to its neighboring country Peru, the Incan empire played a significant role in the formation of Argentina, with numerous empires popping up around the country's vast expanse. During the 16th Century, the Spanish empire was most interested in Argentina, largely due to the country's natural resources. Following the establishment of the Viceroyalty of the Rio de la Plata, the Argentine government rose to prominence and remained the chief government of the land. Similar to the United States, Argentina was founded in 1776 but not yet independent. It would be years before Argentina was officially declared independent. During these years, numerous civil wars sprung up, creating a great disturbance to the growing government. While the civil wars fought to divide the country, they ultimately united the country around the federation once again, with the government declaring Buenos Aires as the capital city.

After the settlement of Buenos Aires as the country's capital city, it seemed that Argentina entered a time of peace, with the government finally able to achieve some stability. During this time, millions of European immigrants flooded the country, seeking its the strong capitalist freedoms. Following the Europeans were a group of Italians who influenced the Argentine culture. To this day, more than 60% of the Argentine culture has Italian ethnicity somewhere in its blood lines. The vast riches of the Argentine government would lead to strong and expedited growth, Argentina quickly jumping into the top ten wealthiest nations in the world. By the beginning of the 20th century, the nation rose to seventh on the prestigious list; however, this moment of financial prosperity quickly fell with the rise of the Great

Depression. With the Great Depression affecting worldwide trade, Argentina quickly entered a stage of underdevelopment that would reduce its wealth to fifteenth in the list of richest nations in the world. While the Great Depression hindered Argentine growth during the end of the century, it would fall even deeper into the recession in the coming days.

With the Great Recession hindering most of the world, Argentina entered a new low with the death of President Juan Perón in 1974. Assuming the throne, Perón's widow Isabel Martínez de Perón declared her authority over the people of Argentina, quickly causing fear and instability to flood throughout the region. Two years later, Argentina's government grew so corrupt that foreign powers began to get involved. With the government slowing to a crawl, the United States sponsored a coup that replaced Perón's leadership with more conservative, specifically right-wing, leadership. This proved to be a terrible mistake on the United States' part as the instilled leadership ruled with brute force and resembled anything but the capitalistic democracy that the United States tried to install. With people being brutally tortured, numerous were murdered and the beginning of the Dirty War was at hand. For the next seven years, right-wing leadership instilled fear into the hearts of the citizens and anyone suspected of adhering to the left-wing ideology was either publicly tortured or killed. Truly, the interference had transpired into an extreme form of conservatism that used any means necessary to establish its ideology. Finally, with the election of Raúl Alfonsín in 1983, Argentina finally had a president who would once again establish equality throughout the country. Following his election, Alfonsín would lead the trial against those who had enacted such terrible crimes against the people of Argentina. To this day, people are still serving life sentences for their aid in the military coup; some have even been executed for their crimes.

From these days on, the government of Argentina returned to its roots as a government that supported its citizens. Today, the government is considered to be the greatest regional power in the Southern portion of South America. The country is a prominent member in both the G-15 and G-20 economies while also joining the boards of the World Bank, World Trade Organization, Union of South American Nations, and the Community of Latin American and Caribbean States. Present at the founding of the United Nations, Argentina has remained a strong proponent of world peace and continually aids in the exposure of corrupt governments worldwide.

To have the greatest experience as a tourist in Argentina, a small portion of the country's history is popular. Only with a true understanding of the economy of Argentina can one truly appreciate the ingenuity of the country's people. Known for being hard-working, the citizens of Argentina are ranked second on the Human Development Index for countries in Latin America. While the history of Argentina is a fascination, the economy of Argentina remains among the most powerful in the world. In 2019, it was revealed that Argentina remains the second-greatest economy in South America.

As a country that is prominent in its array of natural resources, Argentina is among the hardest working countries in the world, its population boasting of have a majority of literate citizens. With a growing gross domestic product, Argentina has proven that its natural resources are not the core competency of the country: rather, its advantage is its citizens. With citizens who are willing to work hard to grow and formulate these natural resources, Argentina is able to find tremendous success and sustainability. Though not the most powerful economy in the world, Argentina has officially been declared a middle-emerging economy, meaning that it is on track to being one of the most powerful and indispensable economies in the world, if its current success is maintained. Though the Argentina's economy appears to be growing steadily, there are some marked weaknesses that are continually monitored by the government. The chief fear is high inflation. In 2017, it the country experienced an annual inflation rate of almost 25%. This inflation rate is markedly higher than the global inflation rate of 3.41%. This signals to economists that the economy's success may be short-lived and that its current success could merely be the results of government interference. While uncertainty exists, the country's economy will be among the most watched in the world, given that its performance is key to most of the world exports and production.

As a country, Argentina is primarily concerned with manufacturing. In 2012, manufacturing comprised 20% of Argentina's gross domestic product. This industry is among the country's fastest growing, seeing 7% growth yearly from 2011 to this day. Beneath the heading of manufacturing, the food processing, beverages, tobacco, and textile sectors dominate this industry. As a relatively mild climate, Argentina's strong growth in rural farms is key to this industry's growth. For tourists looking to glean a history of the Argentine way of life, a stop at the city of Cordoba will lend a glimpse into the primary manufacturing city in Argentina.

In addition manufacturing, Argentina rests heavily on its rail system, building the largest rail system in Latin America. In all, more than 22,970 miles of railway connect Argentina's bustling cities to its mountaintop rural destinations. Tourists to Argentina will no doubt use the rail line at least once during their visit. Additionally, exporters within Argentina also utilize the country's waterways as its second-leading means of transport. At the beginning of the second decade of the 2000s, Argentina's waterways accounted for almost 7,000 miles of transportation routes. The most important port within Latin America is in Buenos Aires, while the port experiencing the most growth is the Up-River port.

While waterways and rail lines connect the country, tourists and other non-residents of Argentina will be forced to utilize the airlines of the country at some point during their visit. Argentina's airports are not as pristine as most of the other airports in the world but there is no shortage of them with 161 airports dotting the Argentine horizon as of 2013. Within Argentina, the largest airport is the Ezeiza International Airport. Each year, almost 85% of the country's international travel is routed through Ezeiza. Additionally, the airport serves as the hub for national airlines such as Aerolíneas and Aregentinas.

Those visiting Argentina will be amazed at the scientific exploration and advancement this country has seen in the past two centuries. Since the award's inception, three citizens of Argentina have won the Nobel Prize in the science category. Perhaps the most notable of these recipients is Bernardo Houssay, the scientist who discovered what the pituitary glands are responsible for the glucose levels of animals. Additionally, Houssay was the first recipient of the award who was from Latin America. In addition to scientific exploration, Argentina has proven its cutting edge technology in nuclear reactors. Inspired by the United States, Argentina became the first Latin American nation to develop its own nuclear reactors in 1957. As the country's nuclear production progressed, it revealed in 1983 that the country had achieved the capabilities of the production of uranium, a key component of nuclear warfare. With the world's focus on peace and disarmament, Argentina declared that its nuclear warfare would only be used for wars and defense. Additionally, Argentina remains a vocal member of the Board of Governors for the International Atomic Energy Agency.

While Argentina remains an active leader for nuclear science, notable advancements in health and medicine have improved health for the entire world. In the early 1900s, Argentine scientist Luis Agote recorded the first successful and safe blood transfusion. Agote's scientific teammate René Favaloro became a leader in the scientific discovery of successful coronary artery bypass surgery. Today, the concept of string theory is being supported heavily by Argentine influences such as Juan Maldacena.

Although the country is heavily supported by the above listed industries, it remains the most visited country in South America, thus establishing the foundation for its tourism industry. In 2013, Argentina saw more than 6 million tourists cross its borders, generating almost $4.41 billion in revenue. The most-visited city in the country remains Buenos Aires. In addition to the numerous cities that create a network of tourism for the country, Argentina also has 30 national parks, many revered as World Heritage Sites. The tourism of Argentina remains the country's primary interest, millions of tourists using planes, trains, or vehicles to progress their way to the southern tip of South America. While South America contains the most-visited tourist destinations in the world, Argentina is a primary supporter of such tourism and should remain on any tourists' list of countries to visit. The proceeding sections of this tour guide will give any tourist the perfect itinerary to follow while also presenting some of the nuances and believed portions of Argentine culture, safety, and food.

A Glimpse into the Culture of Argentina

Tourists visiting Argentina will be treated to one of the more diverse countries in the world. European influences reign heavy in this county, with the most prominent influences being Italy and Spain. The culture of Argentina has been set on maintaining a remembrance of where the country has come from, a dedication that is seen in its dozens of museums. Additionally, there is a tremendous push for the arts in Argentina. With theaters found in every city and bars often the home for startup musical careers, the music industry of Argentina has birthed some of the world's most prominent musicians. The culture of Argentina is best summed in the following quote:

> With the primitive Hispanic American reality fractured in La Plata Basin due to immigration, its inhabitants have come to be somewhat dual with all the dangers but also with all the advantages of that condition: because of our European roots, we deeply link the nation with the enduring values of the Old World; because of our condition of Americans

we link ourselves to the rest of the continent, through the folklore of the interior and the old Castilian that unifies us, feeling somehow the vocation of the *Patria Grande* San Martín and Bolívar once imagined.

The literature of Argentina has been well-respected for numerous years, first coming to prominence in 1550. Over the years, the literature of the country would come to be seen as its own style with works such as *El Matadero* by Esteban Echeverría. Today, Argentina's literature is the result of a movement that began in the early 1800s and culminated in the late 20th century, the Modernist Movement. During the country's rise to prominence through literature, one of the leading activists was Jorge Luis Borges, the man recognized today as being Argentina's most acclaimed writer. As the country saw its literature reach global respect, Borges would be most of the fuel for this fire, looking at the world through the lens of the metaphor.

The most recognized musical genre in Argentina is the tango and rightly so, considering the tango dance found its origin in Argentina many years ago. Further on in this tour guide, the exact city where the tango dance originated will be revealed. Today, tango music is nothing more than a cultural reflection of the country years ago.

Tango saw its prominence during the 1930s to 1950s and is recognized today in various songs within the genres of jazz and swing. Historians and musicians from Argentina note how the music of Argentina has mellowed over the years, hitting its peak with the tango music and now slowly reaching retirement with the mellow yet lively beats of smooth jazz. Today, the most popular musicians still performing tango are Tanghetto, Bajofondo, and the Gotan Project. While the tango music may not be as popular or growing as it used to be, another musical genre that saw its birth in Argentina is growing. Argentina folk music has been seeing more and more people turn from their love for the tango and devote their time to either playing or listening to folk music.

Tourists who have the ability to go to Buenos Aires will be treated to one of the most exquisite theatre cities of the world. With a theater on virtually every corner, the city's cultural history is retold through hundreds of plays and musicals every year. Within Buenos Aires, the liveliest street is Corrientes Avenue, a road that has been named "The Street that Never Sleeps." The most famous theater in Argentina, Teatro Colón, is found in this city and is considered a global leader in performances of both opera and classical performances. Theater first became important to Argentina following the country's first theater, *A Rancheria*, in 1783. This theater was built by Juan José de Vértiz y Salcedo and has since become a legend within the country. A kin to the theater, the cinema has recently become a global success in the movie industry. In 1896, the cinema of Argentina saw its birth and by 1930 it was the leading producer within Latin America. The animated film industry owes a nod to Argentina as the first animated feature films were written and produced there in 1917 and 1918. When compared with the United States, Argentina's film industry looks as though it is underperforming; however, in recent years, Argentina's film industry has seen this flaw and has been working to create higher quality films that can be appreciated globally. As a country, Argentina has received two Academy Awards and seven nominations.

While Argentina's film industry has yet to reach its climax, its contribution from musical scores has been felt globally. Two Argentine composers, Luis Enrique Bacalov and Gustavo Santaolalla, received Academy Awards for Best Original Score. Additionally, Berenice Bejo, an Argentine actress, received Best Actress after she was featured in the film, *The Past*.

One element of Argentine culture that has undoubtedly reached global influence is its visual arts. Today, names such as Candid Lopez, Florencio Molina Campos, and Pio Callivadino adorn visual art exhibits. Within the genesis of art movements, Argentina has been the author of one, the famous Madí Movement that began in Argentina and achieved global success, seeing tremendous influence in the art of the United States. Although Argentina is not considered an artistically rich country, tourists would be remised to miss some of the art that will be covered in subsequent sections.

The Popular Cities of Argentina

With beautiful sunsets, a balmy climate, and a bustling nightlife, Argentina boasts of numerous cities that are yearly destinations for all types of tourists. While any of these cities will satisfy the taste of all tourists, each city is geared specifically towards an individual category of tourist, with some cities boasting of shopping malls galore while other cities more focused on the historical aspect of Argentina. To get a better view of what activities each city finds most appealing, the following section will detail the most popular cities around Argentina while also describing the various activities of which each city boasts.

Buenos Aires

Known as the Argentine equivalent of New York City, Buenos Aires truly never sleeps and the city's nightlife is almost more exciting and inviting than the daily activities. In 2019, the Youth Olympics took place in this capital city, generating more income than the city had seen before. With such prestigious events taking place in this bustling city, every tourist will find something that suits their tastes. Known as the Paris of the South, Buenos Aires offers an array of restaurants and bars to suit the fine tastes of some of its tourists while also catering to the families with numerous attractions that are age appropriate for children. With the cosmopolitan feel of a major city, Buenos Aires also has many neighborhoods with beautiful and quaint homes, giving tourists the ability to be in a destination that holds all of the major amenities of a large city while also seeming like a smaller town. During the nightlife of the city, tourists will be treated to dances originating in Argentina—including the famous tango dance. While the tourist season officially begins in December and ends in February, the mildest temperatures and climate of this region is found between March and May. Tourists should consider coming after the rush of tourists have left the area, a decision that will leave them with more space, more beautiful weather, and more attention as tourists. Alternatively, tourists who enjoy the foliage of their destinations will want to come to Buenos Aires during October or November when the jacaranda trees become most beautiful. Most recently, Buenos Aires has become known for its tasty food and tremendous restaurant experiences. For the tourist who enjoys a mix of leisure and nightlife, Buenos Aires will not disappoint. Because the city is bustling, tourists should plan to reserve every destination well in advance.

Bariloche

Nestled in the Patagonia region of Argentina, the beautiful city of San Carlos de Bariloche adorns the horizon, giving tourists the chance to explore the climate and beauty of Argentina. Tourists who like nature sightseeing will enjoy Bariloche for its mountainous regions that accompany the gorgeous valleys. Known for its ability to host tourists every season of the year, Bariloche is able to accommodate thousands of tourists monthly while appearing to remain a slow and leisure resort. Tourists will enjoy the ability to sail boats, go water-skiing on the famous Lake Nahuel Huapi, or even go skiing down some of the snow-capped mountains that surround Bariloche. For tourists who enjoy slowly meandering down river bends on their own accord, numerous locations support kayaking and boating so that tourists can appreciate the coastal beauty of this city even more. While Bariloche is known for its wide range of activities, it is also known for its chocolate, boasting of more than three dozen chocolatiers in the area. Today, Bariloche bears the title "Chocolate Capital of Argentina." For tourists who enjoy nature, small beauty, and adventure, Bariloche offers the perfect array of activities to ensure they remain busy for their entire visit.

Mar del Plata

While some tourists enjoy setting their own pace while on vacation and exploring as much as they can, other tourists enjoy merely spending their entire vacation relaxing, preferably on a beach. For these tourists, Mar del Plata is the championed destination of their dreams. Known as the best beach resort in Argentina, Mar del Plata boasts of an astounding ten miles of beach. Along these beaches, various activities including surfing, boating, and fishing dominate the tourism industry. With the city being primarily founded on the presence of its beach tourism, Mar del Plata is the unquestioned destination for tourists who are concerned with building a tan while in Argentina. While the beach is the primary destination of this city, there are also numerous museums that offer tourists the chance to grow in knowledge while also relaxing. The most famous museum in the city is the Roberto T. Barili History Museum. For tourists coming to Argentina as a family, Mar del Plata offers the widest array of activities that a family can do together. To compliment the beach and museums, Mar del Plata also houses a zoo, a thriving nightlife, a casino, and a university. Mar del Plata is the perfect destination for families but any tourist will find Mar del Plata to satisfy their tourists' needs.

Mendoza

Argentina is not just about relaxing on a beach or kayaking—it is also one of the world's leading producers of fine wine. For tourists who enjoy seeing the production of wine and attending wine tastings, the sophisticated city of Mendoza will offer the utmost attraction. All of Argentina's wine industry finds its roots somehow in Mendoza. It has been said that while Buenos Aires is the capital of the country, Mendoza is the unofficial capital of Argentina's wine production. Red wine, specifically Malbecs, is Mendoza's popular wine. With numerous wineries offering daily tours and weekly wine tastings, Mendoza offers a rich sense of sophistication that is complimented by the numerous other activities that surround its city. With locations that support paragliding, biking, trekking, skiing, and climbing, Mendoza is among the more expensive yet accommodating tourist destinations of Argentina. Tourists looking to enjoy the finer side of life in Argentina will find Mendoza more than willing to accommodate these desires.

Cordoba

For tourists looking to enrich their knowledge with the history of Argentina, the city of Cordoba offers the perfect destination. Known as the "Heartland of Argentina," this remote city is rich in colonial history while remaining one of the primary tourist destinations of Argentina. Cordoba pays homage to the colonial roots of Argentina with numerous museums and landmarks. Some of these monuments are as old as the 17th century, the most famous being the Jesuit Blocks that were fashioned around this time. The Colegio Nacional de Monserrat campus is found within the city, giving the entire area a unique mix of both history and a desire for learning. The city is located in the middle of a vast expanse of mountains, giving it a markedly "cold" feel despite the climate being the same as the rest of Argentina. For tourists who desire to visit both the natural and man-made landmarks of Argentina, Cordoba offers enough history to keep a tourist interested for days.

USHUAIA

While most of the well-known tourist destinations are found in the larger cities, there is a remarkable beauty found within the smaller villages and cities of Argentina. Ushuaia is one of these cities, known for its quaint feel yet beautiful sites. Nestled in the mountains, Ushuaia offers tourists the ability to go mountain climbing, biking, fishing, and horseback riding. Tourists will enjoy the city's slower pace of activity while also receiving more attention than tourists would in the larger cities. While this city may not attract as many independent tourists, there is never a shortage of tourists. Accordingly, Ushuaia has become a popular destination for cruise ships to momentarily dock. With landmarks such as the Beagle Canal and Cape Horn attracting tourists every year, there is little concern that tourists will exhaust the destinations and activities offered by this city.

Salta City

While the mountains of Argentina attract more tourists than any other destination, the lower plains of Argentina are often the perfect destination for relaxation following days or perhaps weeks of traveling the mountains. One city that is smaller yet growing is the quaint city of Salta City. Salta City is home to some of the earliest indigenous tribes within Argentina and is often visited by those looking to obtain more history than leisure; however, the city is located in close proximity with one of the most impressive clusters of rock in the country. With the rock formation serving as a beautiful tapestry to adorn the sky at sunset, Salta City is worth a quick visit, if for nothing more than a glimpse into the indigenous lifestyle of the country's first inhabitants.

Tilcara

Almost 10,000 years ago, some of the earliest inhabitants in Argentina founded the city of Tilcara, creating what many would later enjoy as a quaint tourist village nestled in the northeastern portion of Argentina. Located in the province of Jujuy, Tilcara is not a bustling tourist destination by any means; however, the destination is located directly in front of the breathtaking Quebrada de Humahuaca, a collection of rock formations that take on numerous different colors. Because the Quebrada de Humahuaca is one of Argentina's most popular destinations, Tilcara is often used as an overnight destination. While not being a tourist city that would keep a tourist busy for days, Tilcara offers the perfect destination for the middle of a vacation to Argentina due to its quant and leisure feel.

PUERTO IGUAZU

Puerto Iguazu offers tourists the perfect destination for photos, with rock formations being complimented by numerous waterfalls around the area. Most of these waterfalls are within the boundaries of the Cataratas de Iguaza, a national park that has more than 250 waterfalls within its borders. Despite its lack of other attractions, Puerto Iguazu is among the most visited locations in the country, bringing in thousands of tourists every year. With the waterfalls forming a natural boundary with accompanying Brazil, the Iguazu Falls is considered one of Argentina's most beautiful locations. In 2019, the Awasi Iguazu hotel opened, giving tourists a prime view of the waterfalls from the comfort of their room. For those who desire the natural beauty of Argentina, Puerto Iguazu will leave any tourist satisfied and most definitely at a loss for words when exposed to the beauty of the waterfalls.

El Chaltén

Following in the footsteps of most of Argentina's tourism, El Chaltén is a mountain enclave that is growing more popular every year. A yearly attraction for naturalists and those in search of Argentina's most beautiful views, El Chaltén offers tourists the prime location for hiking and trekking. Giving credence to the cliché that small things come in big packages, El Chaltén is a small village that supports the yearly tourism to see the accompanying mountain ranges that adorn the Patagonia region of Argentina. For tourists who enjoy hiking to unimaginable heights while also controlling the success of their vacation, El Chaltén offers tourists the perfect place to hike, fall more in love with the source of nature, and see the beauty that this world possesses.

Uco Valley

Known for its ability to produce some of the finest wines in the world, Uco Valley embraces the mantle of sophistication that the city of Mendoza also wears. Uco Valley is the ideal location for couples or single tourists. The sophistication of this valley comes at a steep cost but one that will be justified when tourists are treated to the fine wines for which the valley has become famous. In addition to the wineries, Uco Valley also contains numerous resorts, spas, luxurious hotels, and other attractions that are perfect for tourists looking to focus on their health and relaxation during their vacation. Due to its bustling nightlife and range of adult activities, Uco Valley would not be an appropriate destination for tourists with families.

While this list of cities pales in comparison with the hundreds of other Argentine cities that can accommodate much more specific groups of tourists, these are the cities that are continually voted as the favorite destinations within Argentina. Any tourist visiting one of these cities will find their time in Argentina most enjoyable while also seeing as much as they can.

THE TOURIST ACTIVITIES OF ARGENTINA

The proceeding section of this tour guide will focus on the specific tourist activities that are most popular in Argentina. Without focusing specifically on tourist attractions in Argentina, this section will serve as a guide as to what activities make Argentina the tourism success that it is. At the conclusion of reading this section, tourists will have known what activities they can expect to fill their schedule with while touring Argentina.

HIKING

Perhaps the most exciting and popular tourist activity in Argentina, hiking has become the stalwart of tourism in the country, with virtually hundreds of locations available from which to choose. The term hiking should not be confused with the word trekking, as hiking refers to a day activity while trekking will take days to complete. Additionally, hiking is usually not over incredibly steep inclines while it is not uncommon for those trekking to be involved in climbing rock faces or mountains covered in ice. Tourists who decide to go hiking in Argentina should be prepared for breathtaking views and amazingly lush trails. Among the most popular destinations in Argentina to hike is the famous region of Patagonia. While hiking is popular due to the tourists' ability to act as their own tour guide for the beauty of Argentina, tourists should consider using a trail guide because the mountains are often home to various creatures or nuances that can quickly ruin a vacation. Hikes in Argentina can range from taking a mere two hours to taking an entire day. Tourists who are interested in hiking in Argentina should be prepared for the drastic change in climate that can occur as they make their way from the bottom of a mountain to the peak. Hiking in Argentina has been popular since the country first began experiencing tourism over a hundred years ago. With hiking's popularity growing, the hiking trails in Argentina are usually well-maintained and clearly marked. While hiking is among the most popular activities in Argentina, its successor, trekking, is becoming more popular and will likely outpace it in the near future.

TREKKING

Trekking has become a staple of Argentine tourism, namely because most of the peaks of Argentina are not accessible by a mere hike. With the peaks soaring into the skies, treks are the only way for a tourist to attain their sea level; however, trekking is markedly more dangerous than hiking. With a climate that is home to quickly changing weather, tourists must always be prepared to shelter should one of the famous Argentine storms bear down. When trekking, tourist agencies declare that the first rule of the trek is to remain prepared. For those considering trekking, active exercise should begin months in advance. The average trek will test the willpower and endurance of the most experienced athlete so ensuring one is in the best physical shape is tantamount to the trek occurring both safely and enjoyably. Tourists should prepare for long walks while carrying a large pack, since the weeklong journeys require a carefully selected, albeit heavy, amount of supplies. Tourists should plan to bring a good pair of walking boots that are the dichotomy of efficient: lightweight while not compromising the quality. It is not uncommon for a tourist's boots to be unusable by the end of a trek.

Similar to hiking, tourists should prepare for a wide array of weather situations while on the trek. Experiences such as snow, sunshine, wind, rain, cold conditions, and even hail will plague the hiker during their trip to the peak. For clothing, tourists should wear a single pair of shorts while layering up around the core area. This will ensure that the tourist remains warm despite the rapidly changing conditions. Because there will be a myriad of streams to cross in addition to the rain often present in Argentina, tourists should wrap their feet in plastic bags prior to beginning the trek. Failing to do so could result in the tourist experiencing wet feet that are the gateway to numerous other ailments. Additionally, tourists should pack flannel shirts and a hat and gloves. It is not uncommon for a tourist to experience every climate during the trek. While the threat of snow or rain is contingent on the day, a cold and cutting wind is always present during portions of the trek. For this reason, tourists should pack a lightweight windbreaker. As a precaution against the cutting wind, tourists might also consider bringing hiking poles to provide more stability.

Tourists should also remain alert for strangers during their trek. Because the presence of law enforcement is scarce in the mountains and especially on the peaks, tourists should be wary of strangers approaching them and asking for assistance. Sadly, many tourists have been robbed or injured when they fell prey to a thief's false cry for help. While trekking, tourists can either camp outside or stay in one of the many lodges that dot the horizon leading to the peak. These accommodations are quite economical and are sometimes worth leaving the tent behind for. Additionally, staying in a lodge will afford a tourist the chance to sleep well, eat a properly cooked meal, and attend to any injuries. For tourists who prefer to battle the elements outside, there are numerous campsites that are extremely low cost. Tourists are advised to never camp in a secluded location, as doing so takes them out of the protection of the local law enforcement present at the camp sites. While trekking is among the most exhausting activities in Argentina, there is little doubt that the exhaustion is well worth the tremendous sites that one will see once the peak has been attained.

BOATING

While trekking or hiking the beautiful expanse of Argentina affords tourists the ability to make their own schedules, there are easier and formidable means by which one can tour Argentina. One of the most popular means of touring Argentina is by boat. With rivers dividing the country into small factions, agencies that support touring by boat are numerous throughout the country. Known traditionally as ferries, these boats take tourists either on slow and winding cruises down various rivers or directly to destinations. Tourists using the boat as a means to travel to a destination should consider using the ferries since their cost is almost 20% of what the cost of a private boat tour would be; however, tourists looking to see as much of the coastal or riverside beauty that Argentina has to offer would be best served with a private boating tour. Tourists should always consult their travel agency or hotel to see if the cost of a boating tour or ferry is included in their fees. If not, the average cost of a ferry ride is equivalent to $75. Boating offers tourists the perfect perspective of Argentina that the ground can offer.

Kayaking

Similar to boating, kayaking offers tourists the ability to see beauty that is hidden within the nooks and crannies of Argentina; however, very unlike boating tours, kayaking offers tourists the autonomy and independence of creating their own schedule and traveling at their own pace. Tourists are able to kayak on most lakes and rivers within Argentina and the kayaks are usually available at most bodies of water. Tourist agencies report that the best time of year for kayaking in Argentina is between October and April, effectively including the peak tourist season in this gap. Tourists looking to kayak will be excited by the numerous options that are available to them through the kayaking agencies. Most commonly, tourists will use a kayak for a single day adventure either down a river or around a lake; however, more adventurous tourists will be amused by alternative kayak trips that can see durations of up to sixteen days. While kayak agencies will rarely turn away a potential kayaker, tourists are encouraged to stick to single-day excursions unless they are truly experienced. In addition to longer durations, tourists are also able to choose tour guides from most kayak agencies. Hiring an English-speaking guide is recommended for the day tours as this gives tourists the perfect chance to see the countryside while also learning the history of that area. For tourists kayaking for durations longer than one day, most kayak agencies will mandate the hiring of a tour guide. Tourists are strongly cautioned against undertaking a multi-day excursion without an experienced individual who is bilingual.

For tourists who are going to be in Argentina for an extended period of time, multiple kayaking agencies offer courses that can take even the youngest of beginners and show them the necessary skills for a multi-day kayak trip. For tourists who enjoy the outdoor activities that are less taxing on the body than running or hiking, kayaking is the perfect activity to both see the countryside while also relaxing.

WINE TASTING

Between the rising peaks of the Argentine mountain ranges are miles and miles of vineyards that support Argentina's growing wine production. In all, there are almost 2,000 wineries throughout Argentina, ensuring that no matter the tourist's destination, a winery is in that region. Argentine wine production has been famed for years due to the particular taste that Argentine grapes produce. For tourists who desire the fine sophistication of luxury, one of the many wineries in the area will meet that tourist's needs. With many of the wineries located in valleys, tourists will most likely be required to travel to these locations. To accomplish this travel, there are numerous options. For tourists who are pressed for time and cannot spend as much time enjoying the countryside, traveling by bus to one of the wineries will prove to be the most time-sensitive means of travel; however, many tourists have reported that hiking to the wineries offers the most appreciation for the vast expanse of vineyards within Argentina. Tourists who are coming to Argentina for the wine should consider visiting between June and October. These months afford the most pleasant conditions while also being in the middle of the peak season for production. For tourists who would like to experience multiple wineries in one day, there are numerous wine-tasting expeditions that visit a variety of wineries in the area. Prior to embarking on one of these expeditions, tourists are encouraged to hone their knowledge of wine, as many of the wineries will merely present a wine as it is, not necessarily giving the history or origin of the wine. For those interested in the various wines of the world, Argentina has a vast selection of wines that are exclusive to the country, creating a must-see location for any oenophile.

WALKING TOURS

Not all of Argentina needs to be discovered on the accord of a tour agency or an organized tour. Sometimes, the best tours are self-guided. Other times, a slight hybrid of both styles of tourism is beneficial to the tourists. For tourists who desire the autonomy of controlling the pace of a tour while retaining the historical knowledge and leadership of a guide, the numerous walking tours around various Argentine cities will give tourists the perfect combination. The most popular location for walking tours in Argentina is Buenos Aires with an entire website dedicated to the dozens of walking tours that depart daily around the city. Most of these walking tours are free and inhabited by dozens of tourists, creating the perfect meet-and-greet atmosphere for a tourist. The Buenos Aires walking tours are the #1 ranked walking tours in Latin America. Tourists who want to slowly imbibe the picturesque and historical locations will enjoy taking a walking tour around various Argentine cities.

While there are numerous other activities that tourists have found appealing, the activities listed above can be placed together to create the most eventful and profitable time while in Argentina. Most of the activities listed above are available in the majority of Argentine cities and together, these activities provide a tourist with a cost-effective means of touring Argentina and seeing the numerous locations of the country.

The Climate and National Holidays of Argentina

Tourists to Argentina will find that the country has a wide range of weather conditions that depend on the area of the country. With Argentina being among the longest countries in South America, its climate can be completely different depending on which end of the country one is in. For this reason, the country has been divided into different sections to group the various climates together.

The first area to be explored is Northern Argentina. This area of land is usually like most of South America, hot and dry. From December to March, this area undergoes its wet season and the days are often filled to the brim with humidity. Tourists should avoid this section of Argentina during these months simply because the area's activities slow to a crawl. Often, foggy mornings are only broken up by the frequent rain, after which the fog returns. Most days will reach temperatures upwards of 95 degrees Fahrenheit. Tourists looking to journey to this area of Argentina will be best served during the months of June, July, and August. In the winter months, it is not uncommon for the mountains in this region to be capped with snow, creating the perfect winter getaway for families.

Located in the center of Argentina, Buenos Aires is considered to have the most peaceful and temperate weather year round. Although the summer months of January, February, and March can result in days that have high humidity, the climate of this area is usually quite moderate. With more moderate temperatures, the spring usually experiences days with highs of upper 70s to lows of mid-50s. The summer months usually see highs of 88 degrees with lows around 68 degrees. The nicest time of year to visit is the autumn months, which usually have a tighter range of 73 to 58 degrees. The winter months can grow chilly as the highs shift to 60 degrees and the lows can sometimes reach the lower 40s.

The southernmost region in Argentina is Patagonia, an area known mostly for its exploration. Contrary to the United States, the southern part of Argentina is its coldest climate. Patagonia is home to numerous glaciers, many of which have begun growing in the recent years. From November to March, tourists will find Patagonia very pleasant, with tight temperature ranges that usually linger near the upper 60s to lower 70s. The winters of Patagonia are brutally cold, however; in Ushuaia, the temperature will remain around 0 for almost all of the winter. While the winds of the Southern Andes Mountains cut through the flatlands that surround the mountains, Patagonia is mostly located in a valley, deeming the mountains a sufficient shield against the wind.

As a country, Argentina experiences the normal four season climate just as any other country does. While the seasons may be different than other climates within Argentina due to the change in sea level, all three areas of Argentina will experience the same seasons. While the climate is markedly subtropical in the north, it enters a sub polar climate as the tourist reaches the Tierra del Fuego region in southern Argentina. From December to February, the country experiences its summer months. The months of March through May comprise autumn while the winter months will follow from June until August. In September, October, and November, the country experiences its greatest growth as spring drives the cold winter away. Tourists should bear this in mind as they prepare to tour the country. In terms of the United States' seasons, the seasons of Argentina are markedly opposite. As a country, Argentina's summers are mostly wet and hot with periods of humidity due to the dramatic and sudden shift in temperatures. This is not true for Patagonia as its cold climate causes summer to be the driest season of the year. Tourists are encouraged to travel to Argentina during the winter months when the climate is most mild. Coincidentally, the best climate for tourism coincides with the summer months of areas such as the United States. Though the climate is subtropical, tourists will still experience the peaceful and moderate climate of the country should they tour Argentina in winter.

In addition to having a climate that is contrary to other countries that are north of the equator, Argentina also has holidays that contradict other countries. With some holidays being observed nationally, it is important that tourists check Argentina's calendar prior to travel so that they do not enter during particularly busy national holidays. The following list includes holidays that should be avoided either because of travel by the country's citizens will impede travel or because the specific national holiday will result in closures around the country.

The holiday season of Argentina is kicked off with New Year's Day, which is celebrated on January 1st. Shortly before Easter, the country begins its celebration of Carnival Day. This holiday marks the beginning of the time period that directly precedes the season of lent. With lent contingent on the beginning of Easter, Carnival Day is celebrated on different days every year. Tourists should avoid traveling to Argentina during this time as the streets are usually full of loud and rowdy public celebrations. True to its name, this time usually resembles a circus in the streets. With the religious factions of Argentine culture celebrating the beginning of the season of lent, these celebrations can sometimes become violent. While these events have the propensity to turn violent, they are usually more of a rallying call and a sign of unification than a dividing point. With almost every citizen dressing up in costumes, there is no shortage of festive nature in the air during this time; however, this is a cultural and a national holiday—not one that a tourist could properly celebrate or respect and should therefore not be a reason for touring Argentina during this time.

On March 24, the country holds a national Day of Remembrance for Truth and Justice. This holiday was designed with the victims from the violent Dirty War in mind. Celebrated on March 24, this day signifies the turn in the culture and government of Argentina. The holiday has only been in national remembrance since 2002 when the national Congress made the day a national holiday. Each year this day is set aside to remember the change that occurred following the coup in 1976 that ushered in the National Reorganization Power. As popular as July 4 is to the United States of America, tourists in Argentina during this time will be treated to perhaps the most celebratory day of unification in the calendar year.

Almost exactly one week after the Day of Remembrance for Truth and Justice, Argentina celebrates the Day of the Veterans and Fallen of the Falklands War. This day is set aside each year to remember those who were killed or injured during the violent Falklands War of 1982. Known locally as Malvinas Day, this day is an honor to the 649 citizens of Argentina who gave their life willingly on April 2, 1982, in pursuit of the invasion of the Falklands Island by the army of Argentina. The war lasted 74 days but the remembrance has lasted a lifetime, as many soldiers who fought in this war are still alive and are able to pay tribute to the other men who served and died. The holiday has only been in official remembrance since 2000 when the holiday was enacted to replace the "Day of Argentine Sovereignty over the Malvinas, Sandwich, and South Atlantic Islands." This holiday is observed peacefully, with little disruption to normal life. For the country, it exists as a day to pause and remember the sacrifice made by men so that Argentina could aid a fellow country. Tourists would find the tourist destinations of Argentina to still be operating during this holiday.

Labor Day is celebrated on May 1, contrary to the holiday's observance in the United States. This holiday is set aside to observe the year of labor by the country's citizens and should be avoided by tourists as most of the destinations around Argentina will be closed in accordance with the holiday. On May 25, the national holiday of May Revolution is celebrated, a remembrance of the establishment of the Primera Junta on May 25, 1810, the government that is largely considered to be the first patriotic government within Argentina. This holiday is regarded as one of the most patriotic holidays for Argentina and is celebrated nationally. While tourists will enjoy the patriotic festivities of this holiday, they should be forewarned that most destinations will be closed for this day.

On June 20, Argentina celebrates the Day of the National Flag, similar to Flag Day in the United States. This celebration has carefully been designated for a date that also commemorates the death of the man who created the flag, Manuel Belgrano. Less than one month later, the most sacred of the patriotic holidays is celebrated with Independence Day on July 9. The holiday is celebrated nationally and commemorates the signing of the Declaration of Independence in 1816. This holiday will usually be celebrated for a period of days so tourists with no affiliation to the holiday will want to avoid visiting Argentina during this time. The holiday usually results in most businesses and tourist destinations being closed for two or more days. When this holiday falls on a weekend, tourists should expect closures of up to four days.

From this day until December, there are no holidays that are celebrated nationally on a fixed date.

There are several smaller holidays but these are all celebrated on different days depending on the year. On December 8, Argentina celebrates the Immaculate Conception day, a Christian holiday that celebrates Mary, the virgin mother of Jesus. This holiday is meant to focus on the perceived perfection and holiness of Mary after she was designated as the mother of Jesus. Only three weeks later, Argentina joins most of the world in the global celebration of Christmas on December 25. While Christmas is celebrated for a number of days, most tourist destinations will remain opened since this holiday presents the perfect time for tourists to get out of their country and celebrate the holiday on foreign soil. Tourists will want to check with their tourist agency to see which local attractions are affected by the holiday but should note that most lodging destinations will experience little to no interruption.

The previously listed holidays are an exhaustive list of the immovable and nationally celebrated holidays. Regardless of the holiday, tourists should always check with their tourist agency to see if there are any local holidays taking place that will interrupt or affect their visit. In addition to the national holidays, January 21-29 is the duration of the famous Folklore Festival that takes place yearly in Cordoba. This festival is certain to give any tourist a firm foundation in their knowledge and history of the culture and folklore of Argentina. Perhaps the most famous holiday in Argentina takes place from August 10-23 when the country holds its famed Buenos Aires Tango Festival. Tourists will enjoy the various exhibits of the famous dance and will even be given the opportunity to participate in tangos during the two-week festival. Overall, Argentina has very few holidays that tourists will find an inconvenience. For tourists who are able to visit Argentina during a culture holiday or national observance, they will be privileged to obtain a special glimpse into the personal lives of Argentine citizens.

The Key Attractions of Argentina

Without a doubt, Argentina is home to some of the most beautiful natural and man-made attractions in the world. While some tourists might have a large checklist of attractions to see, it should be noted that Argentina's long length can make things slightly complicated. Tourists should expect to spend entire days traveling if they want to visit a collection of the most popular tourist sites. Over the years, some tourists have found it expedient to merely tour from attraction to attraction, working their way down the country and then flying back home once they reach the bottom of the country. While doing this will eliminate travel time, it does increase costs quite a bit. Whichever way tourists choose to visit Argentina, they should be prepared to either visit attractions that are clumped together or pay a larger price tag to see the most popular places.

Iguazú Falls

Frequently called the most beautiful site in Argentina, the Iguazú Falls is located near the northern tip of Argentina, almost directly adjacent to the country's border with Brazil. The amazing waterfall is located in the center of two national parks that border each other. These national parks are both the same area, simply divided in half by the boundary between Argentina and Brazil. With the waterfall serving as the perfect zipper to unite the two parks, tourists will be able to travel to Brazil and see the waterfall from the Brazilian side as well as the Argentine view of the falls. With the waterfall gaining popularity over the years, Argentina has erected an impressive boardwalk that allows tourists to venture surprisingly close to the waterfall. The network of bridges uses various natural paths in addition to boardwalks and man-made paths to lead customers to a view they will likely never forget. The best possible place to view the waterfall from is a location near the base of the falls called the Devil's Throat. While the Iguazú Falls is seen as one waterfall, the falls is actually a large collection of 190 to 300 waterfalls. Scientists have hesitated to give an exact number since some appear to be quite close to each other yet independent. With the edge of the falls extending for over one and a half miles, this waterfall affords tourists numerous breathtaking sights. With an airport nearby, tourists will find this attraction to be one that can be visited in a day, preferably the day one flies in or on the day before one leaves the area. Regardless of how long one stays at this beautiful location, tourists are certain to be left satisfied by the rush of water and numerous waterfalls.

Los Glaciares National Park

Showcasing the vast differences a tourist will see while touring Argentina, the Perito Moreno Glacier is one of Argentina's primary attractions, a deep contrast to the balmy and humid Iguazú Falls. Considered the main attraction of the Patagonia region, the Los Glaciares National Park centered in El Calafate is a site that will leave tourists with a different appreciation for the monumental ice sculptures that pierce from the murky depths. Tourists will be able to join a cruise or expedition that will bring tourists within touch of the giant glaciers at times. At the center of this park is the Perito Moreno Glacier, one of the world's largest glaciers. At more than 18 miles long, this glacier is easy to see from either the land or the air. The glacier is set within the world's third-largest freshwater reserve, giving tourists the perfect opportunity to glean history in addition to the beautiful sites. With the glacier being located a mere hour away from El Calafate, this glacier is among the most accessible in the world and is home to hundreds of individuals. Tourism around the glacier has grown in years past, with a new visitors center being erected near the glacier's base. The glacier's visitor center offers numerous trips every day that will take tourists on a trek to the glacier's outer walls. While some tourists will be content with merely seeing the glacier and others are merely content with touching it, some tourists seek the thrill of climbing a glacier. Such tourists will be in luck if they visit the Los Glaciares National Park. This park offers daily ice treks on dangerous albeit memorable and breathtaking journeys to the top of the glacier. The average ice trek lasts five hours so tourists should be prepared for an entire day of traveling. While the area is known for its tremendous glaciers, there are other natural monuments that stretch far into the sky, signaling to explorers and visitors where the glacier lies. On one side of the glacier stands the mighty Monte Fitz Roy. This mountain has been called one of the most difficult mountains to climb in the world, most tourists even noting that it places hiking Mount Everest in small competition. In all, the mountain is just over two miles tall and leads tourists on steep inclines before treating them to a magnificent view at its peak. Tourists visiting the glaciers will want to pay an extended visit to this area so that they can take a day trip to either the middle or top of Mount Fitz Roy. Mount Fitz Roy creates the barrier between Argentina and Chile, effectively giving each country a magnificent landmark with which to identify the border. Today, Mount Fitz Roy has fewer travelers than Mount Everest yet it remains just as proud, the loyal protector of the glacier lying miles below.

BUENOS AIRES

The city of Buenos Aires is home to one of the most beautiful manmade structures in Argentina. With the city serving as the embodiment of Argentine culture, there is truly no end to activities to keep tourists busy for any duration. Tourists are encouraged to spend at least one week in Buenos Aires as the beauty and myriad of activities will be a disappointment to miss. To better describe the multitude of events in the city, this subsection will focus heavily on the highest-rated attractions of the city.

While it may seem odd, one of the more visited sections of the city is the Recoleta Cemetery, the cemetery for Argentina's most rich and luxurious. Tourists will be able to tour a small museum that contains relics and souvenirs before embarking on a guided tour. With ornate above-ground graves, tourists will certainly be put in awe by the golden structures that ordain the cemetery. As an added bonus to the cultural hotspot, the cemetery is open to visit at any time of the day and admission is free; however, there are few guided tours so tourists hoping to meander around the cemetery at their own should consider purchasing a low-cost tour guide or map at the souvenir shop. Many of the graves are unmarked so it would be of utmost interest for the tourist to read the biographies of those buried at the cemetery in addition to being given a specific location. Within this cemetery is the shrine of Eva Perón, the famed wife of the deceased president Juan Perón. To this day, it is not uncommon to see flowers laid in abundance at her grave.

Just outside of the city is the beautiful area called Tigre. This delta is known for numerous markets, fairs, and vendors. With the area being primarily located on the river, there is limited transportation to the location; however, the most popular method to travel to Tigre remains the train. At a cost of less than $50 to ride the train there and back, this is also the most cost-effective means. Because this area is frequently a stopping place for tourists, it is best to travel to Tigre on Sunday, when most of the vendors are present. While the vendors may be the area's highlight, there are also numerous museums and even a small park for children. While at Tigre, tourists are also able to rent kayaks or boats to further explore the coastline. Guided tours via boat are available as well. To close out an eventful day at Tigre, many guests will slowly return to the main dock where several restaurants are located. Here, tourists enjoy the Argentine favorite steak and malbec. Malbec is a red wine that is exclusive to grapes that are grown in Argentina. In Argentina, steak is a common favorite and the manner in which an Argentine chef prepares steak is bar none. Tourists will enjoy a steak, red wine, and an evening of local music to close out a day trip to Tigre.

Although Buenos Aires is most known for its tremendous architecture, it is also famous for an art that found its origin in the city: the tango dance. With the tango dance championed in Buenos Aires, tourists must attend at least on milonga before leaving Buenos Aires. A milonga is a night of dancing and frequently, there are multiple milongas every night. These events are well attended and often last well past midnight. With individuals free to come and go as they please, tourists will feel at home either watching the tango dancers parade around the makeshift stages or are free to hop in and begin learning the dance themselves. Locals are always more than willing to aid a beginning dancer in learning the moves, twirls, and steps of proper tango dancing. The most famous milonga occurs weekly on Sunday nights on at Telmo's Plaza Dorrego. Tourists should be prepared to spend a few dollars to obtain admission into one of these events; however, they can be certain that their money will result in what has turned into one of the chief pastimes of Argentine culture. For tourists who do not need the added flare of the milonga at the San Telmo's Plaza Dorrego, there is a free weekly milonga that takes place every Saturday and Sunday night on the La Glorieta.

What is a visit to Buenos Aires without a nod at some of the fantastic art that the country has produced? Tourists desiring the best selection of art should consider attending the Museum of Fine Arts located downtown. The museum is considered one of the best and most complete art museums in the world and contains both art exclusive to Argentina and art from around the world. With pieces from great artists such as Picasso, Van Gogh, Degas, and Monet, tourists can appreciate the fact that the museum is complete free to attend! Because it is large, tourists should plan to spend an entire day at the museum. There are numerous cafes located around the museum should the tourists desire lunch. With a consistent revolution of temporary art displays, there is always something new at this art museum.

Buenos Aires is home to several quaint restaurants that give an authentic glimpse into the country's culture and Café Tortoni is no exception. In business since 1858, this small café has lost no ground and continues to serve only authentic Argentine food. With the café achieving national attention, tourists should expect to wait in line for a bit before being served. Additionally, the café is a bit more expensive than the average in Buenos Aires; however, the experience is like none other. Tourists will be delighted by the glass ceilings designed by Tiffany exclusively for the café. While this location is not one that every tourist has to see before leaving Argentina, it will certainly not leave any tourists disappointed. Nearby, the colorful and lively Feria de San Telmo will keep tourists excited and interested by the hundreds of vendors that are selling items ranging from food stuffs to souvenirs and cooking supplies. Held on Sundays every week, tourists will be treated to a variety of artwork and goods representative of the Argentine culture. Tourists to this attraction should be careful to avoid the pickpockets as this section of the city is simply so overcrowded that theft is rampant. Although the growing threat of theft is reason for a tourist to be concerned, the lack of violence in these areas will leave tourists certain that if they practice common sense and keep their belongings on the front of their body, they can avoid the disappointment and inconvenience a pickpocket can cause.

Another collection of great and authentic street vendors is the Feria de Plaza Serrano. This collection of street vendors is unique in that they primarily offer jewelry instead of goods and souvenirs. Tourists will enjoy picking between various colors of jewelry, adding authentic culture to their wardrobe. After a day of shopping at these street vendors, tourists can cool off with a drink or light refreshment from one of the many bars located directly outside of the street fair.

Tourists in Buenos Aires must check out the Plaza Serrano, a beautiful hub of culture that regularly resembles a fair. The streets of this plaza are usually closed at night so the local bars and restaurants can use them as much-needed spots for tables. The Plaza Serrano is a great place for tourists to simply sit back, enjoy a red wine, and watch the cultural exhibitions around them. With the neighborhood sitting directly adjacent to the west, a nightly ritual for occupants of the street is watching the sun set. In addition to the wine offered on the plaza, there are also a number of bars that offer craft beers, some from the United States. The Plaza Serrano offers tourists the perfect destination to unwind after a long day hiking or sightseeing.

Some of the more unique events in Argentina are the horse races that occur yearly between September and November. These races are available for a nominal fee and are usually well attended so tourists should plan to arrive early. While the polo season takes place between September and November, the horse racing grounds are open year round so tourists can enjoy the beautifully manicured lawns, even if the horses are not there. With the average afternoon housing around five races, tourists fortunate to attend a horse race will see the greatest horses from Argentina compete in either races around the track or rallying games of polo. After viewing a horse race, tourists should consider attending one of the local cafés to partake of a treat that has become a staple of Argentine culture: the empanadas. Stuffed with a variety of items such as beef, chicken, onions, ham, and mushrooms, these fried delicacies are both tasty and quite filling!

Around the city, tourists have raved about eating these at Güerrin, a small restaurant that accepts cash only. For tourists looking for empanadas with a kick, the small café Ña Serapia is a smaller restaurant that serves their empanadas with a side of spicy sauce.

A pinnacle of Argentine entertainment, tourists will find the weekly and nightly shows at the Teatro Colón to be among the most culturally expressive elements in Argentina. With the theater in operation since 1857, this ornate building has seen thousands of plays and has undergone very little renovation. The building is consistently opened for ballets, operas, and even orchestral arrangements. Due to its impressive guest list over the years, this theater is consistently ranked as being in the top five attractions of Buenos Aires. Even if tourists are unable to attend a show, they should still come see the ornate structure standing seven stories tall and occupying an entire block of the city. Within walking distance of the plaza is the famous Botanical Gardens of Argentina, known for its vast collection of statues and tall trees. Unlike most of the botanical gardens of the United States, these gardens are completely free to walk through, an astounding feat considering they lose no beauty with the lack of admission. Within the garden rests a beautiful butterfly house, a manmade lake, a garden dedicated to hundreds of herbs, and even a greenhouse that has been standing for more than one hundred years. The botanical gardens is the perfect place for tourists to share a quick lunch en route to their next destination. With seemingly no end of the grassy fields, tourists will have no trouble finding a location to rest and eat; additionally, the gardens is very relaxed as to what tourists may or may not bring in.

To conclude this subsection on Buenos Aires, one of the more famous locations of the city will be featured: the picturesque neighborhood of La Boca. With each resident seemingly desiring to paint his or her house a vibrant color, the entire neighborhood is a collection of houses that effectively capture the expressive and ofttimes loud culture of the city. Houses that are not being lived in are often given numerous effigies and billboards that showcase Argentine art. At the end of the street is the stadium of the Boca Junios fútbol club, one of the premier soccer leagues of the day. Tourists will want to be sure to stop by La Boca during the day so that they can take photographs near the colorfully painted houses. While Buenos Aires lacks many of the natural landmarks that tourists often desire to tour, this city is the life and soul of Argentina. A trip to Argentina is truly not complete without a few days spent in the "Paris of the South."

Ushuaia

While tourists will find Buenos Aires to be the sole location that has a new activity for any duration of vacation, the more beautiful sites are found elsewhere, notably in Ushuaia. This beautiful expanse of frozen ground allows for beautiful days that give way to gorgeous sunsets as the sun paints a warm glow on the snow-capped mountains before disappearing to rest until morning. Within Ushuaia is the world-famous Patagonia, a collection of glaciers and portions of the Andes Mountains. Of particular interest, Ushuaia is the world's southernmost city and the perfect point from which to embark on a journey to investigate the captivating glaciers. Today, Ushuaia serves as the primary starting point for tours of Antarctica, although its climate is nowhere near as cold as Antarctica's. Tourists will enjoy the ability to investigate the Cape Horn peninsula or walk around the Beagle Channel. Located in the dead center of mountains, glaciers, forests, and even the sea, there is no end of investigation that can take place at Ushuaia. Tourists looking to hike will be excited by the Tierra del Fuego National Park, one of Argentina's national landmarks that boast of exclusive trees and plants. Tourists not afraid of heights should consider touring the San Juan de Salvamento Lighthouse. Built in 1884, this lighthouse has become an icon in this portion of Argentina, known affectionately as the End of the World Lighthouse. Its location, the Isla de los Estados, is accessible by boat for a small fee. Another icon in this location is the End of the World Museum, a museum that will take its guests on a tour of the history of the region. With exhibits dedicated to the indigenous groups that helped settle this portion of land, tourists will be amazed at the rudimentary skills with which the settlers created civilizations in Patagonia. In addition to showcasing the tribes, the museum also has virus exhibits dedicated to the flora, fauna, and animals that exist in this cold portion of Argentina. In the middle of Ushuaia is the famous military prison that was one time housed those guilty of treason. Today, the prison has been repurposed into a museum, the Maritime Museum of Ushuaia. The museum is so large that it is able to house great ships such as the Beagle, the ship used by Charles Darwin in one of his voyages prior to writing his famous book, *The Origin of Species*. Tourists to Ushuaia should not be concerned about the cold climate. Although the country may not be appropriate for elderly or young tourists, it is very accessible by tourists looking for adventure and beautiful sites.

Puerto Madryn

Located on the coastline of the Golfo Nuevo, the historic city of Puerto Madryn was a safe haven for travelers years before it became a hotbed for tourists. Today, the location is considered one of the most secure cities in the world, largely because of its submersion below the rock face of the Valdés Peninsula. Founded in

1886, this location was at one time a deep-water port used by Welsh settlers. With more nature preserves than any other portion of the state, Puerto Madryn has become one of the most famous cruise destinations in Argentina. As the city has grown in popularity, recent years have shown an increase in the national attention this area receives with some agencies even holding water sport championships in the beautiful turquoise waters of the coast. With a strong wind blowing from the Patagonian region that lies due south, there is little doubt that this area contains the greatest expanse of different attractions. Within the city, the Natural Science and Oceanographic Museum is considered one of the premier oceanographic museums in the world. Additionally, this museum is housed in an ornate building that has a clear view of the harbor from the glass windows protecting the front of the building. Within the museum, one of the more famous exhibits is the great skeleton of a whale. While the city offers a wide array of attractions, tourists will be amazed by the cliffs of the Valdés Peninsula, a site that has been deemed protection as a UNESCO World Heritage Site. With an array of different animals and plants, Puerto Madryn offers tourist a collection of different elements of Argentine tourism, all in one place.

Cordoba

Five hours away from Buenos Aires, Cordoba lights up the night sky as the second-largest city in Argentina. While the city is known for its fast-paced night life, the pride of the city is its ornate cathedral, located in the middle of the city. The cathedral is found within the Plaza San Martin and was constructed in 1580. With the cathedral still used sparingly today, it is one of the oldest to still be used for church services. The cathedral's visible beauty is mostly from the late 18th century with some of the paintings inside from the late 1900s. Within the cathedral is a collection of crypts as well, giving tourists yet another aspect of this religious structure to explore. Included in the Plaza San Martin, this location falls under the protection of UNESCO and has been deemed a World Heritage Site. While the cathedral is best visited during the day due to tour times, the cathedral has an exquisite lighting structure that allows for ornate photos to be taken at night.

Tourists coming to Argentina for the first time will find these attractions to be both the most cost-effective and culturally rich destinations. As one can probably see right now, any venturing outside of the capital of Buenos Aires will afford tourists the most beautiful sites of Argentina at a cost: hiking and walking. Tourists should be aware that Argentina replaces the glitzy tourist destinations other country's vaunt with preserved heritage sites and gorgeous mountains. As a country that's length experiences all climates at the same time, tourists will find Argentina to be able to suit their most specific desires.

Staying Healthy and Safe in Argentina

While Argentina offers untold sights and sunsets that promise to leave a tourist wanting to come back, a great trip to Argentina can plummet to the depths of a medical emergency if care is not taken regarding both the health and the safety. In recent days, Argentina has been regarded as being a stable country; however, it still has the violence and hazards that every other country holds. While Argentina is no different in this regard, tourists should be familiar with the threats to the country's safety prior to visiting. The following section will focus on how tourists can ensure they maintain good health while touring Argentina.

Currently, Argentina does not have a wide outbreak of disease; nonetheless, tourists should be properly vaccinated prior to entering Argentina. The Centers for Disease Control recommend that tourists ensure they are up to date on vaccines to fight the following diseases: Yellow Fever, Hepatitis A&B, Typhoid, Tetanus, and Rabies. Even though there is no report of an outbreak, Argentina is accustomed to routine outbreaks throughout its history. In addition to the previously mentioned diseases, there are also diseases carried by the large mosquito population of Argentina. During the wet seasons, any mosquito is at risk for being a carrier of the famous Dengue Fever. The Centers for Disease control recommends that tourists "...prevent against mosquito bites by wearing suitable clothing and liberally applying deep mosquito repellent." The danger with the Dengue fever is that it usually does not show symptoms of being present until it has been alive for ten days. Tourists who begin developing a high fever or aching joints following their visit to Argentina should seek medical attention immediately.

Another threat that was once present in the United States is the Zika Virus. From 2016-2017, there were reported outbreaks of the virus in the United States. Although the disease has not been reported in a few years, it remains a constant threat simply because there is no vaccination for it. Similar to the Dengue Fever, this virus is spread by contact with the mosquitos. Perhaps the most dangerous disease spread by mosquitoes is malaria, a disease that is found in countries directly bordering Argentina.

Tourists need not only be prepared for diseases but also other ailments caused by Argentina's climate. With Argentina being a favorite for tourists who enjoy hiking, the threat of altitude sickness is always present. Tourists should use extreme caution when hiking alone or with a small group. Ascending a mountain too quickly can cause averse affects and have led to the deaths of tourists who were hunting, skiing, hiking, and trekking. Though it should be known through simple common sense, drinking alcohol while climbing is heavily cautioned against. In addition to the myriad of adverse health effects risked in doing so, alcoholic consumption can increase one's risk of altitude sickness. While climbing, tourists should be alert for headaches, lethargy, vomiting, or heart palpitations. These are all symptoms of altitude sickness and a tourist experiencing such symptoms should seek medical assistance immediately.

Tourists traveling to Argentina should be aware of the culture within most medical facilities. Because abject poverty exists in portions of the country, tourists are encouraged to carry cash with them in case they need to seek medical assistance. Most medical facilities will require a small cash payment prior to administering treatment; however, some public health care facilities in the country do offer free care, even for tourists. Tourists on prescription medicine should bring a signed doctors note with the prescriptions listed in case of a medical emergency or if the medicine is stolen. Tourists should also be prepared to reject medical treatment. Many of the medical facilities of Argentina do not carry foreign brand medications, meaning that they will have locally produced medications. Many of these medications have not been vetted properly by a medical organization and most would not pass the standards of western medicine. With this in mind, most would be fine for consumption; however, they will most likely result in negative side effects that could affect the safety of a tourist. For a life-threatening condition, taking the medication is recommended; however, for a medical condition that is merely centered on comfort (such as a non-life threatening reaction, hives, cough, etc.), tourists should exercise caution in taking the medication. As always, tourists should consider buying travel insurance since the medical costs incurred within a foreign country can be cumbersome to deal with in addition to being expensive.

Unlike some of the other countries in South America, the tap water of Argentina is usually fine to drink. The sanitation and hygiene standards of the country have maintained pace with Western civilization. If a tourist ever has a question regarding the safety of water, they can ask "¿Se puede tomar el agua de la canilla?" which translated means "Is the tap water drinkable?" Today, very few tourists get sick because of the water in Argentina but it never hurts to be cautious around the country. If tourists are still concerned about the tap water, there are selections of bottled water available at most every gas station or market. Tourists should be wary for vendors who have bottled water themselves; this method of bottling water lacks almost all hygienic principles and can put a tourist at more risk of getting sick than had they drank the tap water.

Most of the meat in Argentina is cooked to the standards of Western sanitation so tourists need not be worried if they are attending a well-known and reputable restaurant. While hygiene and sanitation are always threats against tourists, there are also numerous threats that involve the tourists' physical safety. The following section will focus on the threats of safety in Argentina regarding violence and theft.

While Argentina is far more advanced than most countries in South America, its close connections with countries such as Brazil, Peru, and Chile have left great influence for those who desire to cause trouble and prey on innocent tourists. Recently, the growth in inflation and unemployment has caused some of the citizens to transgress and become involved in petty crimes. The most common crime in Argentina is bag snatching, also known as petty theft. Tourists will find this crime to be of more nuisance than hurt, as the local police are often powerless to pursue such criminals after the crime has happened. The highest rates of petty crime occurs in areas where public transport is the primary means of transportation. With this in mind, tourists should keep all of their belongings in front of them when they walk. Indeed, this means that even if a tourist is wearing a backpack, the safest means of carrying this backpack is in effect, backwards. Purses should be worn around the neck, not merely around the shoulder, and wallets should be stowed in the front pockets of clothing, not in the back pockets and positively never in a backpack or bag. As a rule of thumb, the more available an item is to a tourist, the less it will be available or easy to steal.

A common ploy around the airports in Argentina is for thieves to disguise themselves as tour guides or taxi drivers. By doing so, they will put tourists at ease when collecting their belongings. After successfully stowing the tourists' belongings in their car, the thief will then drive away quickly, leaving a tourist stranded and possibly without anything except the clothes on his back. To oppose such thievery, tourists are encouraged to only use taxis from a reputable brand or large operation. When leaving an airport or public transportation area, tourists should ignore those asking to aid them in carrying their belongings. Often times, it is not enough to merely ignore the individuals; tourists should become familiar with the phrase: "no gracias," which interpreted means "no thank you." After a tourist says no thank you, true tour aids will cease efforts to help the tourist. Any further help or persistence from a perceived tour guide should be ignored and brushed off. If a tourist feels like they are being pressured at any time, there is a large police presence around public transit areas and officers are more than willing to help foreigners and citizens alike.

Another ploy by thieves is to distract tourists from their belongings. For instance, it has been reported that thieves will sometimes throw mustard sauce or mud at a tourist; when the tourist reacts to the mud and drops their belongings, the thief then rushes up and grabs the items, often never to be seen again. Tourists are encouraged to maintain an itinerary but to keep that itinerary a secret to those who are not family or are not traveling with the tourist. One item that thieves prize above all others is the foreign passport. Passports can be used as identification many times so theft of a passport is usually followed by identity theft. While tourists should ensure that their passports are maintained safely at all times, if they ever do realize that their passport is lost, they should contact the United States embassy in Argentina immediately. The embassy in Argentina can aid a tourist in replacing their passport while also maintaining a lookout for transactions involving the stolen passport.

Another scam that plagues tourists is known as the bar scam. In this scenario, tourists are enticed to enter a bar on the pretense that a free show or a discounted meal will be prepared. Once inside the bar, tourists are not permitted to leave until they pay for a drink that is largely overpriced. Though not as common, tourists have also reported being the victims of carjacking around rural areas. Tourists should remain aware of their surroundings at all times as many of the crimes against passengers of vehicles occur when the tourist is stopped at a stop sign or a red light. Tourists should never get out of their car to confront a violent outburst or an instance of vandalism. Doing so would be to play right into the hands of the potential thieves as they are merely waiting for the tourist to unlock and exit the car. When leaving airports, tourists are encouraged to refrain from packing valuables into their regular luggage. Valuables, a change of clothes, and passports should always be stowed in the tourist's carry-on, which should be connected securely to the tourist until they reach their overnight destination.

Tourists need not worry about terrorist attacks any more in Argentina than they would in their home country. While Argentina has been the victim of some terrorist attacks, these attacks have been mild and are usually in well-populated areas. If a tourist sees anything suspicious, even as a foreigner they are encouraged to call the police using the phone number 101. Sometimes, tourists will be vacationing in Argentina when politics unrest quickly unfurls the banner of tension over the various cities. Protests are not entirely uncommon and are usually directly related to current events: that is to say that they do not happen routinely. Tourists should avoid protests at any cost, even bypassing destinations to avoid protests. Protests in Argentina can become unruly quickly and crime becomes rampant when protesters realize the police are overwhelmed. During these events, it is not uncommon to see guns, barricades, or a massive police presence. Usually, the protests of Argentina remain peaceable but occasionally, protestors will incite violence on whomever they can. Tourists should never watch a protest and absolutely should never join one, even just to make fun of the protesters or have fun. Often, the protestors will broadcast where they are planning protests and often, tourists will be able to find out these locations from the local media. If a tourist is in a portion of Argentina where protests are occurring, it is not necessary to return to the United States immediately. Often, keeping in touch with the local law enforcement or ensuring that the police station's phone number is stored in the tourist's phone will give the tourist the needed confidence to continue their travel.

While violent crimes against tourists are not as prevalent in Argentina, there are reported cases every year of tourists being forced to withdraw sums of money from ATMs. Most of these crimes take place in the large cities such as Buenos Aires. For tourists who find themselves the victims of a crime, there are a myriad of options that can aid them. The first and most prevalent option is the local police, which can be reached by dialing either 101 or 911. Because this will connect tourists with the local police, there may be issues with translation. If the tourist is in Buenos Aires, the police station has opened a 24/7 emergency hotline that will connect tourists with a person who speaks their language. The telephone number for this service is (0800)-999-5000. There is a second multilingual police assistance telephone line issued in Mendoza as well. The number for this service is (0261)-413-2135. As of 2017, the Buenos Aires police station was reporting that kidnappings were becoming more prevalent as thieves saw this as an easier means to obtain money. While this information might frighten tourists, they can be certain that the potential for needing to use any of these numbers is quite low. Often, the local police will be able to assist tourists with petty crime and there are no reports of an American tourist being kidnapped in the past ten years. Tourists can rest assured that the appropriate preventive measures against crime have been taken in Argentina, making the country one of the safest countries in South America to visit.

Staying at the Most Unique Hotels in Argentina

Within Argentina, there are a collection of hotels that have long kept tourists raving about the unique accommodations. While these lodgings are more expensive than the average overnight hotels, tourists should consider spending a night in one of the following hotels.

Voted Argentina's most beautiful boutique hotel, Entre Cielos is a hotel with only sixteen rooms situated within one of Argentina's largest vineyards. Due to its limited accommodations, tourists will need to book this hotel well in advance, sometimes at least two years in advance! In addition to providing an overnight stay, the secluded hotel also has an on-campus spa, a pool, cycling routes that weave between the various vineyards, horse riding, and fishing. Tourists will enjoy fully encrypted wi-fi so they can communicate with loved ones regardless of their location around the world.

Another beautiful and unique hotel is the Patagonia Eco Domes, a collection of individual domes that serve as single accommodations per tourist group. This hotel has only been open since 2001 and is located in the heart of Patagonia. With domes serving as sustainable pads of life for tourists, the eco pods are celebrated due to their lack of pollution and visibility from other sights. The domes are all equipped with their own shower, toilet, fireplace, and overnight accommodations. At the center of these pods is a larger pod that serves as the pods' living room. This collection of pods is the perfect destination for those who have been hiking in Patagonia all day but desire to stay as close to the elements as possible. Despite their secluded nature, each pod is equipped with wi-fi and electricity.

For tourists who desire the comfortability of a five-star hotel while also leaving as little impact on the environment, the Earthship Patagonia is the perfect destination for them. Made almost 100% from recycled materials, this hotel is considered self-sustaining and is as eco-friendly as the hotels come. The walls of the hotel are insulted with recycled rubber from car tires, recycled plastic from soda bottles and cars, and glass from recycled bottles. While the hotel is one of the leading recyclers in Argentina, this hotel loses no beauty by being one of the most eco-friendly locations within Argentina. The hotel's limited accommodations set it apart from the other more upscale unique hotels; however, this hotel is located in a secluded location and is the perfect destination for those who love nature.

Located in the valley between the Pfifter, Norte, and Moyano Mountains, the Estancia Cristina Lodge gives tourists the amenities of a luxury hotel while also allowing them breathtaking views that are not available at any other hotel in Argentina. This hotel is almost a destination in itself, as tourists have to take a bus just to reach the hotel's seclusion from society. Once in the safe arms of the hotel, tourists are able to take a horseback ride to visit the accompanying coastline. Additionally, there are numerous hiking trails around the hotel that are accessible during the daylight hours. With only twenty rooms, this location is sold out well in advance, so tourists should book their room as soon as possible.

For tourists looking to merely rest and relax on their vacation, the Rosell Boher Lodge is the perfect destination. This hotel is located in seclusion in the midst of Agrelo. Each room in this hotel is crafted with tourists in mind. Each room has a roof that can be walked on so guests are able to take in the beautiful sunsets from the comfort of their rooftop Jacuzzi. Maintaining the ability of tourists to exist as autonomously as possible, each "room" of this hotel is actually its own building. Located within close proximity of the famous city of Mendoza, tourists are able to return from daily vineyard tours to

possibly the most comfortable and upscale hotel in all of
Argentina.

Communicating in Argentina

As is true with most countries in South America, Spanish is the primary language in Argentina. Tourists with some fluency in Spanish will be able to communicate on a limited basis. While some Argentinians place their own flare on various words, changing the communication slightly, this comes at no concern to tourists, as these words usually sound similar and can be picked out. In addition to Spanish, tourists will also find that the languages of Quechua and Guarani are spoken by the more secluded groups. During the average tour to Argentina, the tourist will not come into contact with individuals who speak these languages as most belong to indigenous tribes that still live in the mountains.

For tourists who know little to no Spanish, there is no concern for their enjoyment while in Argentina. Listed below is a selection of commonly used phrases that tourists will need to know. Even if a tourist does not know Spanish, there are always bilingual aids around the major tourist sites in addition to smaller and more rudimentary means of communication such as Google Translate. Learning some communication in Spanish will help a tourist expand his cultural image of Argentina while also allowing him to converse more freely with the Argentinians. As a friendly culture, Argentinians love to interact with tourists, making even the smallest of conversations come to life with large laughs and rapid hand gestures. Tourists that take the time to learn even the fewest of Spanish phrases will be loved by the citizens of Argentina. From a practical standpoint, tourists who know some Spanish will be able to communicate better should an emergency arise.

While the list below is a collection of some of the most used phrases by tourists, its pronunciation is not the same as typical Spanish. One of the largest differences between Argentine Spanish and other Spanish dialects is that Argentinians will often leave off the final "s" in the word. Additionally, they roll their Rs differently, creating a different sound that tourists will have to pick up on. With this in mind, tourists should put the following list to memory but should adjust their accent upon their first conversations in Argentina.

"Good Morning" = Buenos Días

"Good Evening" = Buenos tardes

"How are you?" = "Còmo Esta?"

"Fine" = "Muy bien."

"Thank You" = "Gracias."

“I understand” = “Entiendo”

“I don't understand” = “No entiendo.”

“Sorry” = “Perdón.”

“Goodbye” = “Adios.”

“Welcome” = “Bienvenido(a)”

“Thank you”(emphatic) = “Muchas gracias.”

“Excuse me” = “Discúlpame.”

“My name is____” = “Me llamo_____.”

“No thank you” = “No Thank You.”

“Yes” = “Sí.”

“No” = “No.”

“You’re welcome” = “De nada.”

“How much is it” = “¿Cuánto es?”

“It is very cheap” = “Es muy barato”

“It is too expensive!” = “Es demasiado caro”

“Can you lower the price?” = “¿Puede bajar el precio?”

“I would like to buy … this one” = “Quisiera compra eso, éste!”

“I don't like it” = “Aborrezco.”

“I like it” = “Me encanta”

“Money” = “Dinero.”

“I'm just looking around.” = “Sólo estoy mirando”

“I would like to go to…” = “Quisiera ir…”

“Plane” = “Avión”

“Boat” = “Barco”

“Train” = “Tren”

“Taxi” = “Taxi”

“Bus” = “Autobus”

“I would like to rent…” = “Quisiera alquilar”

“Motorbike” = “Moto”

“Car” = “Coche”

“Bike” = Bicicleta”

“Where is …?” = “¿Dónde está?”

“How can I get to …?” = “¿Cómo ir a…?”

"Bank" = "Banco"

"Train station" = "Estación"

"Centre" = "Centro de la ciudad"

"Hotel" = "Hotel"

"Hospital" = "Hospital"

"Is it close" = "Es cerca?"

"Straight ahead" = "Todo recto"

"Left" = "Izquierda"

"Right" = "Derecha"

"North" = "Norte"

"South" = "Sur"

"East" = "Este"

"West" = Queste"

"What time is it? = "¿Qué hora es?"

"When" = "¿Cuándo?"

"Yesterday" = "Ayer"

"Tomorrow" = "Mañana"

"Today" = "Hoy"

"I am here on vacation" = "Estoy de vacaciones"

"I am here for business" = "Estoy aquí por trabajo"

"I am hungry" = "Tengo hambre"

"I am thirsty" = "Tengo sed"

"Enjoy" = "¡Buen provecho!"

"Cheers" = "¡Salud!"

"It was delicious" = "¡Estaba delicioso!"

"What can you recommend?" = "¿Qué recomienda?"

"I am vegeterian" = "Soy vegetariano"

"Not spicy please" = "¡Sin picante!"

"It's too hot" = "¡Es demasiado caliente!"

"I am allergic" = "Soy alérgico"

"Sea food" = "Marisco"

"Peanuts" = "Cacahuete"

"Gluten" = "Gluten"

"I would like..." = "Quisiera..."

"Water" = "Agua"

"Tea" = "Té"

"Coffee" = "Café"

"Beer" = Cerveza"

"Wine" = "Vino"

"The bill, please" = "La cuenta por favor"

"I need to see a doctor" = "Necesito de ver un medico"

"Call an ambulance" = "Llame un médico"

"Where is the hospital" = "¿Dónde está el hospital?"

"I do not feel very good" = "No me siento muy bien"

"It hurts here" = "Me duele aquí"

"Where can I find the restrooms?" = "¿Dónde están los aseos?"

"Help!" = "¡Socorro!"

"Police" = "Policía"

"Danger" = "Peligro"

"I'm lost" = "Me he perdido"

The Food of Argentina

While the sites of Argentina might give tourists breathtaking views, the food of Argentina is truly where the culture and lifestyle mix. Today, Argentina's food front has taken serious charge in the tourism industry and tourists have commented on the great change in food over the last decade. While there is not enough space to write about every good food in Argentina, the list below will highlight the food choices that have brought tourists back to Argentina year after years.

Asado

In the past decade, Argentina has introduced the world to one of its greatest treasures: barbecue. Today, Argentina finds its way to the hearts of many of its tourists via the mouth, and asado is one of the biggest contributors. Asado is known as Argentina's national dish, the dish that has put many a restaurant on the map. The dish finds its heart back in the days of the gaucho, where cowboys would make this meal to combat the cold nights when the sun disappeared. The typical asado is a combination of pork, beef, sausages, ribs, and even sweetbreads that have been kissed by the flames of an open fire. These barbecue pits are most prevalent in Argentina, a calm assurance to tourists that if one is too full for use, there is likely another grill that serves asado. The most famous mixture of asado involves lamb, barbecued to a blackened crisp, and then drizzled with sweet mint dressing.

Chimichurri

The perfect complement to the Argentine asado, chimichurri is a salsa that is made from green plants such as parsley, oregano, garlic, and onions. These vegetables are then combined with chili pepper flakes, olive oil, and either juice extract from a lemon or vinegar. As popular as ranch dressing or ketchup is to the American people, chimichurri has turned many a bland meal into a feast and is able to be eaten with most items in Argentine barbecue. Today, chimichurri is most often used for dipping barbecued meats.

Provoleta

In the United States, a popular dish is the famous grilled cheese sandwich. Tourists will be delighted to find that Argentina has taken this dish and crafted it into a dish of their own with exuberant flavors. The dish is made by combining numerous cheeses into a small pot, melting the cheese and then topping it with flakes of herbs such as chili flakes or oregano. After doing this, the entire meal is grilled, creating a solidified block of cheese that has spices and smooth texture. When served correctly, the cheese will be slightly crusty on the outside but melted thoroughly on the interior. Similar to the asado, provoleta is able to be served with chimichurri and is not expensive.

DULCE DE LECHE

With most of Argentina's agriculture founded on the production and growth of cattle, it is no surprise that most of the country's menu is also decided by what they can use the cows for. With most of the cows producing milk prior to being used for meat production, delicacies such as dulce de leche have become favorites of the country's deserts. Dulce de leche is a fantastic combination of milk and caramel that creates a creamy texture within a crispy exterior. Translated as "milk jam," this delicacy is similar to a cream puff yet the cream is thicker than most interiors. With the dish being wildly popular, it is not surprise that tourists can find this dessert at any local vendors or restaurants. Today, tourists will find the dulce de leche paired with other chocolate delicacies such as salted caramel choc pots, banoffee trifles, and even melted truffles. Paired with a warm cup of hot chocolate or a glass of cold milk, dulce de leche is certain to leave tourists coming back for more.

ALFAJORES

Another dessert that has made its way to the hearts of tourists and citizens alike is the Alfajores. This dish will remind tourists of a cookie sandwich that has a jam filling its center. The cookies are made from shortbread and are often paired with dulce de leche. Some variations of this dish include dulce de leche in the middle of the two cakes of shortbread, creating a chocolate cookie with a shortbread exterior. This cookie is almost as old as the country is, its roots finding their way beyond the country's border to the Arabs. Thousands of years ago, the Spanish people were introduced to the cookie by a voyage from the nearby Moors. This delicacy was then taken on an expedition from Spain to the land now known as Argentina and has since been a staple of the country's tea time or dessert. First introduced by the Moors, this cookie is the best dish to examine the cultural heritage of the foods in Argentina. Since the cookie's introduction, it has seen no changes despite the shift in society and culture since then. Known as the country's national cookie, this delicacy can be eaten alone, dipped in coffee, or even eaten with dulce de leche. After partaking of the cookie, tourists will be pleased to know that its creation is quite simple and can be baked by the tourist even after they leave Argentina.

EMPANADAS

In the early days of the world, the Moors and the Spanish seemed to get along quite nicely, leading to the two countries sharing numerous elements of culture. This included national recipes from each country. In addition to introducing the Spanish to Alfajores, the Moors also brought the famous dish that is now almost synonymous with Argentina: empanadas. Over the years, the empanada has morphed slightly in its appearance but has lost no prestige. The empanada was an immediate success in Argentina, primarily because of the lack of cost associated with its creation. Pairing the affordable contents with a working class that both wanted a portable but cheap dish gave brought the empanada its success. The empanada is created by stuffing meat, beans, or other wholesome foods into a breaded exterior. This combination is then either baked or deep-fried, creating a crispy biscuit that is filled with protein. Today, the empanada will be created differently depending on the province in which it is created. In addition to the meat-filled empanadas, tourists will also find that there are variations that contain sweet stuffing and are served as a dessert. The dessert empanadas are typically filled with jam, cheese, or dulce de leche. After the dessert empanadas have been cooked, it is common for them to be sprinkled with cinnamon, sugar, or raisins, depending on the province and season. Tourists will have the opportunity to eat an empanada at almost every meal, considering every vendor has their own variation of the delicious dish.

Matambre Arrollado

True to Argentine form, if there is a way to create a new dish based on steak, the country will come up with it. Tourists should try matambre arrollado, a slim slice of meat that is grilled and then filled with various ingredients such as other meats, vegetables, and a variety of spices. This dish can be thought of as a snack and the literal interpretation of its name means "hunger killer." Today, this meat creation is usually eaten by workers who cannot take a break for a meal while working. The meat's compact nature allows it to be taken virtually anywhere. While some associate this dish with the poorer working class, tourists will enjoy the spicy nature of this dish.

Yerba Mate

Argentine dishes fall into three categories: dishes imported from other countries, tasty dishes that the country has created in the past hundred years, and cultural dishes. Yerba mate is one of the oldest dishes in the country, first reported being served with the South Americans used the herbs to fight sickness in their camps. After the indigenous dwellers of Argentina saw the powerful taste and affect of the herbs, they used them to make a drink that has aided the Argentinians in staying healthy during the wet seasons. This drink is also very high in caffeine, which has aided its popularity. The process of creating the drink begins by taking dried yerba leaves and crushing them into a fine powder. After this, the leaves are dissolved into hot water and then available for consumption. Alternatively, yerba petals can also be steeped into the drink similar to teas. The most popular means by which one drinks yerba mate is by placing the drink into a gourd and then using a metal straw to consume the contents. With such a great cultural drink also comes cultural reflection; the drink is often passed around the group, allowing each person to sip the drink. After the drink has been sipped by everyone, the owner of the drink is permitted to drink the yerba as their own. Tourists will be amazed at the strong yet soothing taste and texture of the yerba mate.

CHORIPÁN

While it has not been mentioned extensively in this tour guide, the sport of fútbol is tremendously successful in Argentina and its province has changed the way of life for the citizens of Argentina in many ways. One of those ways is in the food eaten before and after the games. One of the staples of pre-fútbol matches has become the spicy tang of the choripan. This less than delicate food is the barbecue of the tailgate in the United States and is commonly eaten before and during the various gaming matches of the country. Comprised of either pork or beef, the choripán is usually grilled over a fire, the most authentic vendors trading the false flame of a charcoal fire for the sear of the flames created by a wood fire. Once the meat has been grilled, it is usually split open, sliced down the middle, and then stuffed with various vegetables. Most vendors will place chimichurri in the middle, the green salsa adding the perfect measure of zest to the spicy meat. This meat combination is then topped off by being placed between two pieces of crusty bread, some using whole wheat bread and others using white bread. Some vendors will add pickles and peppers to the mix as well; however, even if these are not added directly onto the sandwich, most vendors will have these available for free at their station. Tourists given the opportunity to try the choripán will not be disappointed by the perfect combination of smoked meat and spices.

CARBONADA

While Argentina's climate does not lend it the greatest market for soups, the country does experience some cold months during which the following soup will be of utmost pleasure. Carbonada is a very popular dish in the southern provinces around Patagonia simply because of the hearty foundation the soup creates in addition to being a warm refreshment following days out in the cold. Classified as a stew, Carbonada is made from the combination of meat, potatoes, corn, peppers, bacon, carrots, and numerous fruits that widely depend on the province from which one hails. Similar to the eating style of yerba mate, carbonada is properly eaten when placed in a pumpkin and sipped directly from the pumpkin. Some provinces will even place these ingredients directly into the pumpkin and allow it to stew, infusing the taste of the pumpkin with the myriad of flavors already present in the stew. Ironically, some provinces will even spoon portions of carbonada into an empanada, effectively creating a soupy burrito that is immensely filling. Carbonada is also popular with low-income areas since its ingredients can all be switched out for different, cost-effective ingredients. Out of all the foods listed in this tour guide, tourists will have the hardest time finding carbonada since it is very much a seasonal food and even considered a regional food. Today, the stew is considered the most portable stew in the country and is a favorite of hikers.

UNA MUZZA

While tourists may think this food is similar to the dish of their country, pizza in Argentina takes a very different look than tourists will recognize. Apart from the typical circular shape and the composition of dough, there is little that tourists will recognize about the pizza. Following Argentina's desire for bread, the pizza of the country often has very high crusts, sometimes exceeding two inches thick. As a general rule, the thicker the pizza crust, the thinner the pizza sauce. The main ingredient of

Argentine pizza is mozzarella cheese. Often, an entire piece of pizza will be covered in the cheese, making it impossible to see any other ingredients in the pizza. After a healthy portion of mozzarella cheese has been evenly spread across the pizza, chefs will then add traditional favorites that change depending on the province. Some of the favorites that are usually accepted across the entire country are green olives, oregano, or chili flakes. After the pizza has been baked, it will be served as traditional pizza would in the United States; however, it is not referred to as pizza. The citizens of Argentina actually refer to this dish as una muzza. Within cities that have shown a propensity to follow Western tradition such as Buenos Aires, tourists might even find una muzza bars around the city. These bars will sell the dish by the slice, giving tourists the perfect chance to test una muzza and see if it measures up to their expectations. A compliment to the una muzza, vendors will often sell a faina with the slice of pizza. The sole purpose of the faina is to soak up the excess cheese, thus creating a cheesy bread to follow the eating of the una muzza. While there are some textural differences between pizza and its variation, tourists will recognize the dish immediately and will be sure to fall in love with the cheesy variation of the American staple.

Milanesa

Within the poor and working class, Milanesa has become a popular dish due to its cheap ingredients. Fashioned from the excess beef from the outside of the leg, this dish's prime ingredient is silverside. With silverside being among what many would discard after cutting up the cow, it is very low cost, allowing Milanesa to be made regularly and for a fraction of what steak costs. To make the silverside edible, the vendor will take the silverside, hammer it repeatedly and then coat its exterior in bread crumbs. At this point, the dish fails to be anything more than cheap meat that honestly, tastes very cheap; however, it is with the addition of spices and other toppings that this dish truly comes to life. With seemingly each province creating their own variation of this dish, there is no end to the different styles of Milanesa and tourists are certain to find one that meets their expectations. Some variations include adding a fried egg to the top while others coat the entire exterior with cheese. One variation that tourists may not like as much is the la suiza, which is fashioned from topping the meat in gruyere. This dish is often served with French fries, a salad, and a sauce that is fashioned from ham, tomato sauce, and cheese. Milanesa will not suit everyone many tourists have remarked that its flavor tends to be markedly different than what they expected; however, tourists have also confirmed that this is among the tastiest dishes in Argentina. At such a low cost, tourists will lose little if they choose to try this dish.

LLAMA

Indeed, Argentina adds to its list of exotic meats with the introduction of llama steak. For tourists who can overcome the thought of eating one of the many creatures that dot the Argentine horizon, they will be treated to one of the most delicate steaks in the world. Within Argentina, the meat has become commonplace for those seeking a healthy alternative to the steak. This is largely due to the lower fat levels of the llama. While it is an alternative to the more unhealthy meats such as steak and chicken, tourists have confirmed that its flavor bears the definition of "earthy." The most common dish in which llama is served is the famed empanada; however, some restaurants will serve a llama steak as a delicacy of the restaurant. Llama is not one of the "must-try" dishes of Argentina but if tasted, will leave tourists with a greater glimpse into the true culture in Argentina.

HUMITA

Perhaps the most noticeable element about the dishes of Argentina is their ability to either be the main dish or to be an accessory to the meal. Additionally, most of the meals are also able to be eaten on the go so that the workers can continue working while eating. One such dish is humita, a hearty meal that is essentially corn mash. The locals make this dish by mashing corn with milk, onions, goat cheese, and a variety of spices. This combination is then, packaged between two leaves, and then steaming or boiling the meal until the mash is a thick gooey consistency. Humita is one of the few dishes that has stood the test of time, records of its existence dating as far back as the pre-Colombian era. Today, the dish is most common in cities surrounding the Andean Region of Argentina. Additionally, this dish is enjoyed in surrounding countries such as Chile, Peru, and Bolivia. Another hearty dish that is exclusive to the country is locro, a thick and warm stew that is made more exclusive by its limited availability. Locro is a seasonal dish, made available only on May 25 in remembrance of the May Revolution that aided Argentine independence. Locro is comprised of beef, pork, tripe, white corn, and red chorizo. Depending on the province the dish is being served in, it is not uncommon for other ingredients such as cumin, pumpkin, squash, and bay leaves to be added to the dish. Tourists would find locro to be very similar to dishes such as carbonada.

MEDIALUNA

The final food that will be revealed in this travel guide is arguably the finest and most refined dish that has been presented yet. Available at only select coffee shops, the medialuna resembles what most of the world refers to as a croissant bun, hence the name luna. This breaded delicacy is light enough to be enjoyed with any drink while also being heavy enough to dip into your strong Argentine coffee. Its breaded interior allows it to be a great snack for in between meals. Paying attention to the heritage of the dish, the medialuna is commonly eaten as a breakfast food or as a midday snack with tea and coffee. Because there are similar foods that cost less, the medialuna is a refined dish that is usually only eaten by the privileged few. Tourists will want to split a medialuna and experience the buttery goodness while in Argentina.

There is no doubt that there are dishes exclusive to a certain province that were not included in this tour guide. The dishes listed above will give a tourist the best eating experience while in Argentina. Additionally, the foods listed above are among the "safer" foods to try in Argentina. Tourists can be certain that the foods listed, if prepared correctly, will all have a good taste that is sure to leave the tourist wanting more Argentine cuisine on their next trip to Argentina.

Final Thoughts on Argentina

As the sun slowly descends over the Andean Mountains, tourists are treated to a myriad of color exploring across the sky. Truly, the most beautiful moments in Argentina come when the world slows down to pay attention to the beauty that nature can produce. Within this tour guide, hopefully the attitude and hard work of Argentina has been conveyed. Argentina has its flaws but tourists can be rest assured that they will be treated with utmost respect while touring Argentina.

References

Hamre, Bonnie. "Most Popular Cities in Argentina." *TripSavvy*, TripSavvy, 3 June 2019, www.tripsavvy.com/popular-cities-in-argentina-1636643.

O'Higgins, Sorcha. "The 15 Best Destinations to Visit in Argentina in 2018." *Culture Trip*, The Culture Trip, 23 Nov. 2017, theculturetrip.com/south-america/argentina/articles/the-15-best-destinations-to-visit-in-argentina-in-2018/.

Klene, Julie. "Patagonia Trekking Guide: Everything You Need to Know." *Intrepid Travel Blog*, 25 June 2019, www.intrepidtravel.com/adventures/trekking-advice-patagonia/.

"Your Guide to Hiking in Argentina's Patagonia." *Class Adventure Travel*, 26 Sept. 2018, www.classadventuretravel.com/your-guide-to-hiking-in-argentinas-patagonia/.

Luongo, Michael T. "In Argentina, Touring the Tigre Delta." *The New York Times*, The New York Times, 24 Nov. 2010, www.nytimes.com/2010/11/28/travel/28tigre-overnighter.html.

Simm, Carole. "Kayaking in Patagonia, Argentina." *USA Today*, Gannett Satellite Information Network,

15 Jan. 2019,
   traveltips.usatoday.com/kayaking-patagonia-
   argentina-58335.html.

"Argentina Wine Regions: The Ultimate Guide to the
   Top 5 Region." *Bookmundi.com*,
   www.bookmundi.com/t/argentina-wine-
   regions-the-ultimate-guide-to-the-top-5-region.

"Free Walking Tour Buenos Aires: Every Day. No
   Booking." *Free Tour Buenos Aires*,
   www.buenosairesfreewalks.com/.

Trimble, Michaela. "Is This South America's Most
   Beautiful Wine Region?" *Vogue*, Vogue, 16 Mar.
   2017, www.vogue.com/article/argentina-wine-
   region-travel-guide-malbec-torrontes.

Dwyer, Helen. "Weather in Argentina - from Subtropical
   to Sub Polar." *Chimu Adventures Blog*, 11 Sept.
   2019,
   www.chimuadventures.com/blog/2016/09/wea
   ther-argentina/.

Alex. "Holidays Celebrations in Argentina." *Expat Blog
   Argentina*, 26 May 2018,
   vamospanish.com/discover/argentina-
   holidays/.

"25 Best Things to Do in Buenos Aires (Argentina)." *The
   Crazy Tourist*, 26 Jan. 2020,
   www.thecrazytourist.com/25-best-things-
   buenos-aires-argentina/.

"10 Top-Rated Tourist Attractions in Argentina:
	PlanetWare." *PlanetWare.com*,
	www.planetware.com/tourist-
	attractions/argentina-arg.htm.

Jennings, Allyson. "Health and Hygiene Tips for
	Argentina." *World Nomads*, World Nomads, 8
	Apr. 2019, www.worldnomads.com/travel-
	safety/south-america/argentina/argentina-
	health-and-safety.

"Southamerica.travel Llc." *SouthAmerica.travel Our
	Name Is Our Passion*,
	www.southamerica.travel/Argentina-
	Tours/Country-Info/Staying-Healthy-in-
	Argentina/.

Lonely Planet. "Health in Argentina." *Lonely Planet*,
	www.lonelyplanet.com/argentina/health.

"Passport Services." *U.S. Embassy in Argentina*,
	ar.usembassy.gov/u-s-citizen-
	services/passports/.

"25 Best Things to Do in Buenos Aires (Argentina)." *The
	Crazy Tourist*, 26 Jan. 2020,
	www.thecrazytourist.com/25-best-things-
	buenos-aires-argentina/.

Crisis24. "Argentina: Increase in Kidnappings in the
	Buenos Aires Region." *GardaWorld*,
	GardaWorld, 14 May 2017,
	www.garda.com/crisis24/news-

alerts/62446/argentina-increase-in-kidnappings-in-the-buenos-aires-region.

"Guide to Argentina: How to Stay Safe in Argentina." *CHOICE*, CHOICE Australia, 19 Nov. 2018, www.choice.com.au/travel/destinations/argentina/articles/safety-guide.

Tmb. "Argentina Travel Tips: TMB Travel Health Advice." *TMB*, 3 Nov. 2015, www.tmb.ie/blog/argentina-travel-tips.

"Unique Hotels in Argentina." *Unique Hotels in Argentina | Mostuniquehotels.com*, mostuniquehotels.com/searchresults.php?Search=Argentina.

Moseley-Williams, Sorrel. "10 Dishes Every Visitor to Argentina Needs to Try." *CNN*, Cable News Network, 10 July 2015, www.cnn.com/travel/article/10-argentina-dishes/index.html.

"The Most Important Vocabulary to Know during Your Trip in Argentina." *Evaneos.com*, www.evaneos.com/argentina/holidays/survival-vocabulary/.

Amigofoods. "17 Delicious Argentine Food Dishes You Should Be Eating in 2019." *Amigofoods*, 25 Aug. 2019, blog.amigofoods.com/index.php/argentine-foods/argentine-food-dishes/.